THE FRENCH REVOLUTION

ADRIAN GILBERT

W
FRANKLIN WATTS
LONDON•SYDNEY

This edition 2003

Franklin Watts
96 Leonard Street
London
EC2A 4XD

Franklin Watts Australia
45-51 Huntley Street
Alexandria
NSW 2015

Illustrations   David Frankland
Designer   Billin Design Solutions
Editor   Caroline Brooke Johnson
Art Direction   Jason Anscomb
Editor-in-Chief   John C. Miles

A CIP catalogue record
for this book is available
from the British Library.

Dewey classification: 944.04

ISBN 0 7496 5195 4

Printed in Hong Kong/China

THE FRENCH REVOLUTION

CONTENTS

A revolution represents a dramatic change in the way people live their lives. Usually this means the government of a country is violently overthrown. Political power is seized by one group from another to create a new social order.

> **"The Third Estate does all the work that the privileged Estates refuse to do. Well-paid and honourable positions are reserved for the privileged."**
>
> From Abbé Sieyès's book, *What is the Third Estate?*

REVOLUTION

Although England had a revolution during the Civil War (1642-49) — when Parliament took power and beheaded the King — it was not as far-reaching as the French Revolution. The King, Louis XVI, was executed, the nobility abolished and the Church's powers severely reduced. Such was the drama of these events that even at the time people called it a "revolution".

THE ESTATES

But before we can analyze why and how the French Revolution occurred, we need to look at the old political and economic system — the *Ancien Régime* — that existed in France before 1789, and that was so dramatically swept away in the years of turmoil. Then, the population of France was divided into three unequal groups called Estates.

The First Estate comprised the clergy. It owned large areas of land but was not required to pay taxes, although a sum of money (*don gratuit*) was sent to the government each year. As well as bishops, who generally enjoyed a luxurious lifestyle, the clergy also included a large number of poor parish priests who lived and worked among ordinary people.

Of these, many were keen to see a change in the system of government. The nobles (aristocracy) of the Second Estate paid few taxes and enjoyed many privileges, including hunting rights over peasant lands and the better jobs in the government and army. Some nobles were prepared to accept reform, but others were determined to maintain or increase their rights.

LOUIS XVI

Coming to the throne in 1774, Louis XVI (1754–93) was a conscientious monarch, although he preferred hunting and eating rather than carrying out his official duties. When the Revolution began, Louis angered the people by repeatedly going back on his word. Above all, he failed to understand that he would have to accept a new type of government, so that in the end, Louis XVI lost his crown and then his head.

The Third Estate contained all the rest of society, ranging from poor peasants and urban workers through to lawyers and businessmen. They paid the bulk of the nation's taxes, but had little say in how the country was governed. This unfair system caused resentment, and, for some, a desire for change.

Â faut espérer q'eü Jeu la finira ben tôt.

Un Païsant portant un Prélat, et un Noble,

Allusion aux impots dont le poids retombait en entier sur le peuple: M.M. les Ecclesiastiques et les Nobles non seulement ne payoient rien, mais encore obtenoient des graces, des pensions qui épuisoient l'Etat, et le Malheureux cultivateur pouvoit apeine fournir à sa subsistance.

This Revolutionary engraving shows a peasant carrying a nobleman and a priest.

Causes of the Revolution

Although Ancien-Régime France was a very unfair society, so were most societies in Europe, and yet they did not experience a revolution in 1789. The French Revolution occurred as a result of a large number of social, economic and political causes coming together at the same time.

> "It is very remarkable that in every conversation bankruptcy is the topic. The curious question is would a bankruptcy occasion a civil war and a total overthrow of the government?"
>
> **English writer Arthur Young, travelling through France in 1787**

NEW IDEAS

During the 18th century France underwent a change in the way people thought they should live within society. Important writers of the day, such as Voltaire and Rousseau, began to question the old traditions of total obedience to the monarchy and the Church. A new intellectual movement developed, known as the "Enlightenment". It stressed the importance of reason over tradition. Although some historians now question the importance of the Enlightenment as a cause of the Revolution, it did create a climate of debate that encouraged people to think for themselves.

FINANCIAL CRISIS

A more serious and direct cause of the Revolution was the financial crisis facing the French government in the 1780s. The government was spending far more money than it received in income, and it was forced to take out vast loans to cover the difference.

To prevent the country from going bankrupt, the finance minister, Charles Alexandre de Calonne, attempted to extend taxes to the clergy and the nobility. Not only did they not want to pay tax, but they also resented the King and his government interfering in their affairs.

To make matters worse, France was experiencing an economic slump. As well as a general depression in trade and industry, the country had suffered a series of bad harvests in the 1770s and 1780s. The prices of many essential foods — especially bread — increased, but people's wages failed to keep up with this rise. As a result, social discontent spread through both towns and rural areas. By the spring of 1789 rioting had broken out across much of the country and the army was placed on permanent standby.

As France faced breakdown, the call was made for a session of the *Estates General*. This meeting of representatives from the three Estates would attempt to resolve the country's difficulties.

CHRONOLOGY

1775-83 France spends vast sums of money aiding the American colonists fighting the British in the war of the American Revolution.

1786 Calonne attempts to introduce tax reforms.

1787 The Assembly of Notables – made up of nobles and senior churchmen – rejects Calonne's proposals to extend and reform taxation.

1788 8 August: The decision is taken to hold a meeting of the Estates General.

1789 April: Riots break out in Paris and in the countryside. 5 May: The Estates General assembles in the royal palace at Versailles.

FACT FILE

CAUSE AND EFFECT

• 1786 – French government income is 475 million livres but expenditure is 587 million livres

• During the 1780s around half of all government expenditure goes on paying interest to those who have lent it money

• 1788–89 – As a result of the bad harvest, bread prices rise by 50 per cent in some areas (for the poor, bread forms at least three-quarters of their diet)

• April 1789 – French troops are called in to suppress a demonstration by paper workers outside the Réveillon factory in Paris

• Between 1752 and 1780 Denis Diderot publishes the 35 volumes of *The Encyclopedia*. This work aims to provide readers with a sound knowledge of the world based on reason alone

• France is divided up into internal customs areas, which means that, in many cases, customs duties for goods passing through the country have to be paid several times over

As the deputies of the three Estates made their way to the first session of the Estates General, most knew that some sort of change was inevitable. But at the time no one could have imagined that this was the first step towards full-scale revolution.

> **"Yes, truly we shall be free! Our hands will never wear shackles again."**
>
> **Ernest Duquesnoy, a member of the National Assembly**

NATIONAL ASSEMBLY

The middle-class deputies of the Third Estate — mainly professional people such as lawyers and minor government officials — wanted a new constitution that would give them some real power and a role in the running of the country.

By contrast, Louis XVI saw the Estates General as a means of raising extra money and he had no interest in changing the nature of his government.

The Third Estate's dismay at the King's attitude turned to anger when the nobility blocked proposals for political reform. As a result, the leaders of the Third Estate decided to turn their backs on the nobility and clergy, and on 17 June they adopted the title of the National Assembly. This new institution claimed to act on behalf of the French people. It encouraged members of the other two Estates to join them as equal members.

A substantial minority of liberal nobles and sympathetic clergymen joined the National Assembly. By doing so, they gave added authority to the Assembly and undermined the power of the King.

THE OATH

On 20 June, the members of the National Assembly turned up to their usual meeting hall but found it locked and guarded by troops. Outraged at what they saw as an attempt to suppress the Assembly, the members marched off to a nearby tennis court. Here, they swore a solemn oath "never to separate" until a fair government had been set up.

This was a turning point in the Revolution — it was a direct challenge to the King's authority.

CHRONOLOGY

1789 5 May: The government opens the Estates General.
6 May: Debate over voting procedures.
13 June: The first clergymen join the Third Estate.
17 June: The newly formed National Assembly states that voting should be done by head (and not by separate Estates as many aristocrats want).
20 June: The Tennis Court Oath is signed.
24 June: Most of the clergy (mainly parish priests) decide to join the National Assembly.

The drama of the Tennis Court Oath, as depicted by Jacques-Louis David.

MIRABEAU

The Comte de Mirabeau (1749–91) was one of the nobles who sided with the National Assembly. His powerful personality and skill as an orator soon made him a leading figure in the Assembly. Mirabeau favoured a moderate approach, in which the King and an elected government worked side by side. His death through illness in 1791 robbed the Revolution of one of the most influential voices for moderation.

FACT FILE

THE GREAT FEAR

• During the summer of 1789, many peasants are afraid that rich landowners are hoarding grain to starve them into submission. As a result, a wave of paranoia (the Great Fear – *Grande Peur*) sweeps through much of France. Peasants attack the larger estates and burn rent records

To the Revolutionaries who besieged it on 14 July 1789, the Bastille prison was a potent symbol of repression.

In July 1789 the Revolution became increasingly violent as Louis XVI began to draw up plans to crush the National Assembly by force. But the ordinary people of Paris intervened and thwarted the King's plans.

ROYAL CONTROL DETERIORATES

Louis XVI ordered the army to concentrate its forces around Paris, but the King could not be sure of the loyalty of many of his regiments. The rank-and-file soldiers had suffered the same hardships as the rest of the population, and as morale and discipline deteriorated, soldiers began to mix with civilians.

> **"You may consider the Revolution to be over, since the authority of the nobles has been utterly destroyed."**
>
> **Gouverneur Morris, later US Ambassador to France, writing to the American President immediately after the fall of the Bastille, 1789**

DESMOULINS

A lawyer turned journalist, Camille Desmoulins (1760–94) played an influential role in encouraging the people to take direct action against the King. On 12 July he called upon them to search for muskets and gunpowder, the first step in the march on the Bastille. He later became a close associate of the Revolutionary leader Danton, and was executed with him in 1794.

RADICAL REVOLUTIONARIES

Radical Revolutionaries warned the ordinary people of Paris — called *sans-culottes* because they wore ordinary trousers and not fashionable knee breeches (*culottes*) — that the King was a threat to the Revolution. They encouraged the sans-culottes to seize weapons and defend themselves against royal control.

FALL OF THE BASTILLE

On 14 July 1789 a vast crowd marched on the prison-fortress of the Bastille, where the government held a store of arms and ammunition. For most Parisians the Bastille was a symbol of royal repression, a place where innocent people had been imprisoned for years in its dark dungeons — often without trial.

The Bastille's defenders consisted of a few nervous soldiers, and when one discharged a musket, the crowd surged forward, breaking down the gates and killing the governor.

Two days after the fall of the Bastille, the Minister of War informed the King that the army could not be trusted to support the monarchy. This was another crucial turning point in the Revolution, for the King and his government relied on force as the ultimate means to stamp out any unrest.

The fall of the Bastille confirmed that power had passed from the King to the National Assembly and its increasingly radical supporters.

CHRONOLOGY

1789 12–17 July: Repeated riots in Paris.
15 July: The electors of Paris form their own local government, the Commune.
5 October: Parisian market women lead a march on Versailles to protest to the National Assembly about food prices.
6 October: The King is brought back from Versailles to Paris, followed by the National Assembly.
10 October: The National Assembly decrees Louis XVI "King of the French".

FACT FILE

EVENTS OF 1789

• By early July the strength of French troops in and around Paris rises from 4,000 to 20,000 men

• The most reliable troops in the French army are Swiss and German mercenary units, which have not been affected by Revolutionary ideas

• When the sans-culottes break into the Bastille they find just seven prisoners

• After the fall of the Bastille large numbers of French nobles begin to emigrate from France. During the summer of 1789 20,000 *émigrés* flee abroad, the vast majority bitterly opposed to the Revolution

• Rioting in Paris spreads to other cities and to the countryside, and new local governments are formed throughout France

The majority of the members of the National Assembly originally hoped to work alongside Louis XVI in what is known as a constitutional monarchy, where the king has influence but real power lies with an elected government.

> **"[It is like] the spectacle of young schoolboys mad with joy because they are promised an extra day's holiday."**
>
> The Comte de Mirabeau, commenting on the disorder he encountered in the National Assembly

THE RIGHTS OF MAN
Although Louis XVI reluctantly accepted the presence of the National Assembly, he did his best to obstruct the new government. Setting up the government was not an easy task either, with the country in a state of near-constant turmoil. The Assembly itself was poorly organized, and was characterized by an atmosphere of passionate argument and unruly behaviour.

The first key measure adopted by the Assembly was the formal abolition of the old feudal system.

This was followed by the *Declaration of the Rights of Man and the Citizen*, a document setting out the basic principles of the new order. The Declaration stated that "Men are born free and equal in their rights," and went on to guarantee basic liberties, the right to a proper trial, freedom to express opinions, fair taxes and the protection of property.

MONEY PROBLEMS
Short of money and keen to limit the influence of the Church, the Assembly seized the vast lands owned by the Church and sold them off to raise funds. More controversial, however, was a reform called the *Civil Constitution of the Clergy*, which placed the Church under the authority of the government. Clergymen were to be elected by local assemblies and swear allegiance directly to the State. Since many priests believed that religion and the State should be separate, their relationship with the National Assembly became increasingly bitter.

CHRONOLOGY

1789 4 August: Feudal rights are abolished.
26 August: Declaration of the Rights of Man and the Citizen.
2 November: Church property is nationalized.
19 December: Paper money – notes called *assignats* – is issued by the National Assembly.

1790 13 February: Suppression of religious orders (except those engaged in teaching).
19 June: Abolition of the titles of the nobility.
12 July: Publication of the Civil Constitution of the Clergy.

FACT FILE

THE NATIONAL GUARD

• The lawlessness in Paris (and the country) leads the Assembly to organize a military force to back up its authority. Under the leadership of a liberal noble, the Marquis de Lafayette (1757–1834), the Paris city militia is reformed as the National Guard. Although intended to be a force to deal with any royalist plots, the National Guard's other major function is to protect property from the actions of the sans-culottes. Subsequently, however, poorer citizens are allowed to join the National Guard, and as a result it becomes increasingly radical

NO EASY SOLUTION

For all its fine words, the National Assembly was unable to solve the country's economic problems, especially the food shortages. While radicals encouraged the people to blame the King for their problems, the King further increased his unpopularity by attempting to block the new laws.

The Marquis de Lafayette fought with French forces during the American Revolution and later became leader of the National Guard.

Outbreak of war

The other countries of Europe had shown little interest in the early stages of the French Revolution, but during 1791 relations between France and the rest of Europe began to deteriorate.

> "Our liberty can only be assured in so far as it has a mattress of corpses on its bed. I am willing to become one of its corpses."
>
> **Statement written by a student volunteer in 1792**

WAR IS DECLARED

There were many reasons for the outbreak of war. Austria and Prussia thought that a short war against France — a traditional enemy — would be to their advantage, although by 1791 they had also become concerned at events in Paris, fearful that revolution might spread to their own countries and overthrow their governments.

Louis XVI also encouraged war, hoping that a French defeat would overthrow the Revolutionary government. He encouraged the Austrian emperor and other foreign leaders to come to his aid.

Some French generals, including Lafayette, hoped for a successful war, as victory would make them personally more powerful. Early in 1792, France declared war on Austria and later on Prussia.

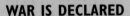

DANTON

Like many Revolutionary leaders, Georges Jacques Danton (1759-94) was a middle-class lawyer. An early member of the Jacobin Club, his skill as an orator brought him political success, and he became the guiding force in organizing French resistance to the foreign invasions of 1792. A leading voice in the call for the King's execution and the destruction of the Girondins, he later became sickened by the excesses of the Terror.

The defeat of Prussian forces at the Battle of Valmy, as depicted in a contemporary engraving.

WAR INTENSIFIES

Prussian and Austrian armies invaded France during the summer of 1792, and the collapse of French forces caused panic among the Revolutionaries in Paris. A mob of sans-culottes invaded the Tuileries palace, massacred the King's Swiss Guard and imprisoned the Royal family.

The National Assembly then suspended the King's rule. In August, a powerful Prussian army led by the Duke of Brunswick prepared to attack Paris. Inspired by the new Minister of Justice, Danton, the government rushed soldiers to the front.

PANIC AND FEAR

Meanwhile, Parisian radicals exploited the panic in the city. In the belief (untrue) that jailed prisoners were threatening a counter-Revolution, many were killed in what became known as the "September Massacre". Although the Prussians and Austrians were defeated, the war made the Revolution increasingly violent.

CHRONOLOGY

1792 20 April: War is declared.
25 July: The Duke of Brunswick issues a manifesto threatening Paris with total destruction if the Royal family is harmed.
10 August: The sans-culottes invade the Tuileries palace.
2–6 September: Prisoners are massacred in Paris.
20 September: The Prussians are defeated at Valmy.
6 November: The Austrians are defeated at Jemappes.
19 November: The Edict of Fraternity is issued – a French offer to the peoples of Europe to provide assistance in any uprising.

INCREASING HOSTILITY

• Although intended to frighten Parisians, the Brunswick Manifesto, in fact, enrages them and makes them increasingly hostile to the King

• After the attack on the Tuileries on 10 August, 600 loyal Swiss Guardsmen are killed by the mob. Some are thrown from balconies on to the pikes of the sans-culottes below and their severed heads are used by children as footballs

• The National Assembly's decree, "la patrie en danger" (the homeland in danger), issued on 11 July, is a call to arms for all Frenchmen to fight the enemy

• A patriotic song written by Rouget de Lisle is taken up by Revolutionaries marching to Paris from the port of Marseille, and soon becomes the French national anthem, "La Marseillaise"

• Of the 1,200 prisoners killed in the September Massacre, most are clergy who have refused to accept the Civil Constitution or else minor criminals

Execution of the King

When the Revolution started, few people wanted the end of the monarchy or the King's death. But Louis XVI's refusal to accept change, the advent of war and the growing power of the radicals proved fatal to the monarchy in France.

THE FATE OF LOUIS XVI

In June 1791 the Royal family attempted to flee from France, but they were captured at Varennes and brought back to Paris. This escape attempt further undermined Louis' popularity, and by 1792, once the country was at war, calls were made for him to stand trial.

The people suspected that Louis XVI was secretly communicating with foreign powers to send armies to restore him to power. Their fears — subsequently proved correct — were strengthened by the increasing emigration of nobles, many of whom were busy organizing armed forces to invade France. These suspicions led to the attack on the Tuileries palace in Paris on 10 August 1792 and Louis' imprisonment.

The moderates of the Third Estate, who had dominated the National Assembly, were losing power to the radicals, who appealed to the sans-culottes to take direct action on their behalf. The Assembly began to fall apart under pressure from radical members within its walls and from sans-culottes demonstrations without.

LOUIS XVI IS BEHEADED

The National Assembly was replaced by the more radical Convention which, on 22 September 1792, confirmed the abolition of the monarchy and the beginning of Year One of a new French Republic.

After long deliberation, the Convention decided to make the King stand trial. He was found guilty and, by a narrow majority, sentenced to death. The Convention rejected any appeal, and on 21 January 1793 Louis XVI was executed.

CHRONOLOGY

THE FLIGHT TO VARENNES

20 June: At nightfall, the King and Queen and their two children — heavily disguised — slip out of the Tuileries palace to a waiting coach.

21 June, morning: The escape of the Royal family is discovered by the Revolutionary authorities. Orders are immediately issued for their recapture.

22 June, evening: A postmaster recognizes the Queen in disguise and the Royal coach is apprehended in the town of Varennes.

23 June: The Royal family begins its trip back to the Tuileries. To keep order, an official poster is issued. It reads: "Anyone who applauds the King shall be flogged. Anyone who insults him shall be hanged."

"I die innocent of all the crimes of which I have been charged and I pardon those who have brought about my death."

The last known words of Louis XVI, spoken on the scaffold

The executioner Sanson displays Louis' severed head.

MARIE ANTOINETTE

The Austrian princess Marie Antoinette (1755–93) was married to Louis XVI as part of a dynastic pact between Austria and France. Her Austrian ancestry made her unpopular with the ordinary French people, however, and when news of her extravagance with public money became common knowledge, dislike turned to hatred. A determined woman, Marie Antoinette was a leader of the Court party and loudly and foolishly encouraged Louis to resist reform of any kind.

• On being told that the poor have no bread, Marie Antoinette is reputed to respond, "Well, let them eat cake!" The statement, however, is almost certainly untrue

• After the suspension of his rule, the King is called simply Louis Capet – Capet being the surname of one of his ancestors

• The guillotine is introduced into France by Dr Joseph Ignace Guillotin (1738-1814), on the basis that it is a more effective and humane means of execution than the traditional axe, which can take several blows to remove the head

• The guillotine is first used in France in April 1792, and thereafter becomes the standard means of execution

• After Louis XVI's execution, spectators rush forward to dip handkerchiefs into the blood dripping down from the scaffold to keep as souvenirs. One souvenir hunter, on tasting the blood, exclaims: "It is vilely salt!"

Revolutionary groups

There was never just one single Revolutionary movement in France. The leaders (and the led) came from different backgrounds and had different motives for wanting change. And during the course of the Revolution, people's attitudes shifted and new political groups gained influence and power.

> **"The Jacobin Society is the great investigator that terrifies all aristocrats, redresses all abuses and comes to the aid of all citizens."**
>
> **Camille Desmoulins, writing of the role of the Jacobins in 1791**

LIMITED DEMANDS

In 1789, the Revolution was dominated by liberal aristocrats and the middle-class from the Third Estate. Their demands for change were limited. They wanted to restrain the power of the Royal government, make the taxation system fairer and have a degree of political power, but this demand was to be restricted to property owners.

Although many aristocrats wanted to keep the old system more or less as it was, a substantial group of nobles — such as Mirabeau and Lafayette — believed that the *Ancien Régime* was not working properly and was detrimental to the overall good of the country. They were prepared to give up some of their rights in return for a better system of government.

SANS-CULOTTES

During 1789, the Revolutionary leaders feared that the army might crush the Revolution. To prevent this, some Revolutionaries called for support from the predominantly working-class sans-culottes of Paris. In return, the sans-culottes demanded a say in the running of the country, an end to the King's rule and new laws to protect them from economic hardship.

These demands ran counter to the wishes of the moderate middle-class Revolutionaries, who were now trying to limit the Revolution in their favour.

They were too late. The Revolution was taking an increasingly violent course, especially after the outbreak of war in 1792. New political groups and parties came into being, most hostile to each other.

IS THAT A FACT?

RURAL REVOLUTION

Although the Revolution was centred primarily in Paris and a few of the major cities, the bulk of the population consisted of peasants living in the countryside. They initially supported the Revolution because they wanted to abolish the rights the nobility had over their small landholdings. But they opposed many of the more radical measures, especially the attack on the Catholic Church. Throughout the Revolutionary period, there was tension between town and country.

REVOLUTIONARY CALENDAR

In October 1793, the Convention adopted a new calendar. This was part of the movement to replace Christian symbols with something considered more appropriate for Revolutionaries, and was based on the seasons of the year. The year began on 22 September (the date of the declaration of the French Republic in 1792) and consisted of 12 30-day months, each with three 10-day weeks (the remaining five days were set aside for national holidays).

Vendémiaire (Vintage)
22 September–21 October

Brumaire (Mists)
22 October–20 November

Frimaire (Frosts)
21 November–20 December

Nivôse (Snow)
21 December–19 January

Pluviôse (Rains)
20 January–18 February

Ventôse (Winds)
19 February–20 March

Germinal (Buds)
21 March–19 April

Floréal (Flowers)
20 April–19 May

Prairial (Meadows)
20 May–18 June

Messidor (Harvest)
19 June–18 July

Thermidor (Heat)
19 July–17 August

Fructidor (Fruits)
18 August–16 September

Sans-culotte Revolutionaries dance around a tree topped by a "cap of liberty".

COMINGS AND GOINGS

• After the attack on the Tuileries on 10 August 1792, the moderate military leader, the Marquis de Lafayette, attempts to march on Paris and restore a constitutional monarchy, but his troops desert him and he flees into exile

• Of the many clubs and factions that operate in Paris, the most moderate are the Feuillants. They hope to develop a constitutional monarchy, but are swept aside as the Revolution gains momentum

• The Girondin faction want to make a clean break with the past, which includes the suspension of the King's powers and the formation of a French Republic

• The Jacobin Club develops into one of the most radical organizations operating within the Convention. Its members include Danton, Desmoulins, Robespierre and the extremist agitator Jean-Paul Marat

• The sans-culottes represent the politically aware working class of Paris. They believe in direct action and popular democracy (where all men have the vote), and are prepared to use force to achieve their aims

A Revolution for all?

Although the leaders of the French Revolution talked a great deal about liberty, equality and brotherhood, they did not necessarily believe that these advantages should be extended to everyone.

"The deed is done. The monster is dead."

Charlotte Corday, after assassinating Jean-Paul Marat

A LIMITED REVOLUTION

Most Revolutionary leaders were white, middle-class and male, and their chief concern was to ensure that they gained and kept political and economic power for themselves. Other groups could be given a degree of legal freedom, but not much else. As a consequence, the French Revolution was a limited revolution, especially for other groups, such as the working class, women and black people.

The more radical Revolutionaries — such as the Jacobins — were prepared to give voting rights to almost all men. But when the Jacobins lost power at the end of 1794, the new moderate leaders of the Revolution insisted that the vote should only be given to men with property. The Revolutionary leaders also prevented the workers and peasants from forming their own associations or trade unions, which they feared might create disorder and act as rivals to the Revolutionary government.

WOMEN'S VOICES

Although a number of women did play an active role in the Revolution, it was never even considered that they would be given the vote. Some feminists, mainly allied with the most radical groups, did hope to ensure greater participation for women, but after the suppression of extremists in 1793, they lost influence.

ABOLISHING SLAVERY

France had colonies in the West Indies, such as San Domingo, with plantations worked by black slaves. While some Revolutionaries wanted to free all slaves, most were only prepared to free slaves in France and not in the colonies. Slavery was finally abolished in all French possessions on 4 February 1794.

TOUSSAINT L'OUVERTURE

Pierre Dominique Toussaint L'Ouverture (1746–1803), a former black slave, played a leading role in a slave revolt in the French colony of San Domingo. A brilliant soldier and skilful politician, he gained control of the island, subsequently repelling attacks by the Spanish and British. However, his attempt in 1801 to make San Domingo independent led to his imprisonment by French forces under Napoleon.

Parisian women marched on Versailles in 1789 to demand that the King should move to Paris.

CHRONOLOGY

1791 14 June: A law is passed – *Loi le Chapelier* – which prohibits the formation of workers' associations and the right to strike.
22 August: Beginning of a slave revolt in the French colony of San Domingo (now Haiti).
27 September: The abolition of slavery in France but not its colonies.

1793 29 September: The Law of the General Maximum attempts to help the economic plight of workers by regulating prices and wages. It is not a success, however.
30 October: Women's political clubs are closed down by the Revolutionary authorities.

1794 4 February: The abolition of slavery is extended to all French colonies.

The Reign of Terror

Following Louis XVI's execution early in 1793, a struggle developed between the more moderate Girondins and the radical Jacobins. Among the Jacobins was a new rising star of the Revolution, Maximilien Robespierre.

> ## "Robespierre is extremely suspicious; he sees treason everywhere."
>
> Jérôme Pétion, Mayor of Paris

JACOBINS DOMINATE

In the contest between the two factions, the Jacobins outmanoeuvred the Girondins. They looked beyond the debating chamber of the Convention to draw in radical sans-culottes, whose threats of violence were used to intimidate moderate members of the Convention. Following a series of violent mob demonstrations early in May 1793, the Girondins were charged with being enemies of the State and were expelled from the Convention. Many were imprisoned and later executed.

The Jacobins now dominated political life in France, and they transferred power from the Convention to two tight-knit groups, the Committee for General Security and the Committee of Public Safety. The key figure in the Committee of Public Safety was the enigmatic and calculating Robespierre, who gathered around him a band of devoted followers who included Georges Couthon and Louis de Saint-Just.

THE TERROR

A combination of French military defeats in the spring of 1793 and renewed plots from counter-Revolutionaries caused a surge of mistrust among the Jacobins and their supporters. This marked the beginning of "the Terror": government through fear and violence, intended to eliminate all opposition by whatever means.

The Law of Prairial allowed courts to convict people without hearing any evidence, and the Law of Suspects allowed the government to put people in prison without trial. In this atmosphere of fear, a simple denunciation was sufficient to send a person to the guillotine.

CHRONOLOGY

1793 29 May–2 June: Fall of the Girondins.
27 July: Robespierre joins Couthon and Saint-Just on the Committee of Public Safety.
24–31 October: The trial and execution of Girondin leaders.
5 September: Terror is declared "the order of the day."

1794 14–24 March: The arrest, trial and execution of the radical Hébertistes.
30 March–5 April: The arrest, trial and execution of Danton and his supporters.

OPPOSITION CRUSHED

By the end of 1793 the threat of revolts within France and of foreign invasion were over. Although this made the Jacobin-led Revolution safe from attack, unity within the group broke down. By skilful manipulation, Robespierre was able to destroy all opposition — first, the extremely radical Hébertist movement and then the more moderate Indulgents, led by Danton and Desmoulins.

The guillotine – defining symbol of "the Terror".

ROBESPIERRE

A hard-working lawyer, Maximilien Robespierre (1758–94) was called the "incorruptible" because of his honesty and his inflexibility in personal and political matters. He was obsessed with the need for virtue in government, and he eliminated anyone who stood in his way. To safeguard what he believed to be the right course for the Revolution, he was even prepared to send innocent people to their deaths. Robespierre was a man who rose to the top through his energy and dedication to the Revolution, but he made himself many political enemies.

FACT FILE

THE TERROR

• Saint-Just's cold and heartless manner earns him the title of the "Angel of Death"

• In the port of Nantes, nearly 2,000 people, condemned for activities against the Revolution, are taken out in barges to the mouth of the River Loire and drowned. The tying together of men and women to prevent their escape is referred to as a "Republican marriage"

• One estimate suggests that there are 17,000 official executions during "the Terror", while total figures (including deaths in prison and executions without trial) number around 50,000 deaths

• *"Tricoteuses"* ("knitting women") are working-class women who attend sessions of the government in Paris and are officially permitted to knit during these sessions. They also sit and knit around the guillotine while executions are carried out

• Before being guillotined, Danton tells the executioner to show his head to the crowd as it is "well worth having a look at"

Revolution restrained

Following the elimination of his major rivals, Robespierre was free to impose his authority on the Revolution. However, this dominance was to be short-lived.

SANS-CULOTTES LOSE THEIR POWER

Robespierre had relied on the sans-culottes in his bid for power, but now that this goal had been achieved, he no longer needed them. Troubled by their unruly behaviour, Robespierre eventually imprisoned and executed a number of the sans-culottes' leaders.

In the process, however, Robespierre and his associates began to isolate themselves from popular support — their power was now based on terror alone.

Other members of the Convention resented Robespierre's dictatorial powers and, fearful for their own safety, they sought an opportunity to get rid of him.

THE FALL OF ROBESPIERRE

They did not wait long to strike. During a debate on 26 July 1794, a surprised Robespierre found himself under attack by several Convention members. News of this event spread through Paris, leading to a sudden and powerful upsurge of opposition to him.

The following day, a newly confident Convention voted for the arrest of Robespierre, knowing that few sans-culottes would come to his aid. Robespierre and his followers were seized in an event known by its Revolutionary calendar name of Thermidor. They were swiftly tried and guillotined. In the space of just two days, Jacobin rule had been overthrown.

The Convention had to face renewed unrest, however, especially from the very poor and the sans-culottes who suffered great hardship during the severe winter of 1794-95. Fearful that demonstrations might lead to a re-emergence of the Jacobins, the Convention brought in the army to crush street protests.

Within the Convention control was handed over to a group of five individuals, collectively known as the Directory, who ruled France until November 1799.

> **"You monster spewed out of hell. Go down to your grave with the curses of the wives and mothers of France. The thought of your execution makes me drunk with joy!"**
>
> **A woman shouting to Robespierre on his way to the guillotine**

A MORE STABLE GOVERNMENT

While the Directory was in power, attempts were made to put the country on a more secure economic footing and to repair some of the damage caused by years of turmoil. The Directory was helped in this task by a series of good harvests and a measure of financial stability.

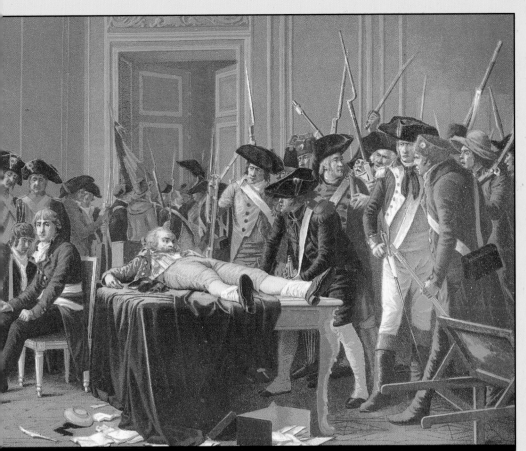

Robespierre's arrest. He tries to commit suicide by shooting himself, but fails.

MORE TERROR

• After the fall of Robespierre new fashions develop, including hairstyles cropped at the back as if in preparation for the guillotine. Some people even wear blood-red silk ribbons around their necks

• In the south and west of France, the reaction to "the Terror" is particularly violent. Several thousand people who have supported the Jacobins are killed in a "White Terror" between 1795–97

• An *émigré* force, supported by the British, lands at Quiberon Bay in Brittany in June 1795, but it is defeated by regular French troops led by General Hoche

• Between 1796 and 1798, the French armies achieve great success against their enemies, conquering the Netherlands, the Rhineland, Switzerland and most of Italy. The army becomes an increasingly powerful force in French political life

• As a reaction to "the Terror", the sons of rich Parisians, called "*jeunesse dorée*" ("gilded youth"), form gangs that attack sans-culottes

CHRONOLOGY

1794 28 July: The execution of Robespierre and his associates.
30–31 July: The Committee of Public Safety is reorganized.
12 November: The Jacobin Club is closed.

1795 1 April: Germinal – a demonstration by sans-culottes for cheaper food and greater freedom.
20–23 May: Prairial – an armed uprising by the poor demanding food and the release of political prisoners. The uprising is put down by the French army, and its leaders are imprisoned or executed.
5 October: Vendémiaire – a third uprising in Paris is suppressed by regular troops under the command of Napoleon Bonaparte.

1799 9–10 November: Napoleon seizes power in the coup of Brumaire.

Consequences

The French Revolution was one of the great turning points in history. Even at the time, people were aware that momentous changes were taking place, and since then historians have argued endlessly over its causes and consequences.

> **"Never was any such event so inevitable yet so completely unforeseen."**
> **Alexis de Tocqueville, writing on the Revolution**

A MIXTURE OF CAUSES AND MOTIVES

The many causes of the Revolution included the spread of more sceptical attitudes towards authority, the emergence of a politically ambitious middle class, general resentment because of an unfair tax system and nobles' privileges, and the near-bankruptcy of the French government.

The various Revolutionaries — ranging from liberal aristocrats to radical Jacobins — had a mix of motives for wanting change. And during the Revolution the aims of the Revolutionaries changed from a fairly modest reform of the tax system to the formation of a new Republic.

WINNERS AND LOSERS

To a considerable degree, the French Revolution can be seen as a middle-class uprising, in which those with wealth and education did best. Other groups both gained and lost from the Revolution. The Church was a clear loser, with most of its lands sold off and its influence diminished.

Although some 1,200 nobles were executed and many others forced into exile, most of the nobility survived the Revolution. The peasantry as a whole gained from the ending of feudal dues, and while the poorer peasants suffered from inflation, the better off bought up Church and other confiscated lands, and gained political power in the new institutions of local government.

WHAT ABOUT THE POOR?

The urban poor suffered great economic hardship before, during and after the Revolution. But through the example of the Jacobin sans-culottes, the oppressed had at least been given a vision of what was possible if the masses took direct action. This possibility played an important part in the development of Socialism, the political philosophy behind so many of the revolutions of the 19th and 20th centuries. In this way, the French Revolution acted as a model for future revolutions around the world.

IS THAT A FACT?

A VIOLENT WORLD

The violence of the Revolution is often emphasized over other significant factors. The brutal deaths of approximately 50,000 people cannot easily be ignored. However, to put this into perspective, a similar number of people died in Ireland during the uprising of 1798, and following the Russian conquest of Warsaw, perhaps as many as 45,000 were killed in a single day on 4 November 1794.

THE DECIMAL SYSTEM

One of the lasting achievements of the Revolution was the standardization of the cumbersome system of weights and measures of pre-Revolutionary France. The French Academy of Sciences tried to provide a rational, yet natural, basis of measurement: the metric system was adopted in 1795, and the metre became the basic measure of length.

The excesses of the Revolution are lampooned by British cartoonist James Gillray.

FACT FILE

TURMOIL AND CHANGE

• The old overlapping system of local goverment from the *Ancien Régime* is replaced by the department system, one that remains to this day

• The conflict between State and Church is resolved in the 1801 Concordat (agreement) between the Pope and Napoleon, which states that the Catholic Church would be the religion of the "majority of Frenchmen". Other religions are also tolerated

• Most modern historians now believe that the turmoil of the Revolution held back the development of French trade, agriculture and industry, thereby giving Britain a vital lead in the Industrial Revolution

• After the defeat of Napoleon in 1815, Louis XVIII is put on the throne. In 1824, he is succeeded by Charles X, who attempts to return France to the ways of the Ancien Régime. He is overthrown in the Revolution of 1830

• Europe was convulsed by more revolutions in 1848 – most of them influenced by the French Revolution

Glossary

Ancien Régime
The political and social system that existed in France before the Revolution. Royalty, the nobility and the clergy enjoyed many privileges over the rest of the population — the Third Estate.

assignat
Paper money (notes) issued by the Revolutionary government. During the course of the Revolution they lost much of their value due to inflation.

clergy
Members of the First Estate, who carried out the religious duties of the Church.

Committee of Public Safety
A committee set up by the Convention in 1793, which developed into the centre of power within the Revolutionary government.

Commune
The local government of Paris, generally radical in outlook.

Convention
The Revolutionary government that replaced the National Assembly on 20 September 1792 and lasted until 26 October 1795 when it was, in turn, replaced by the Directory.

counter-revolutionary
A person or group acting against a revolution.

coup
The sudden seizure of power by an individual or a small group.

don gratuit
The payment — "free gift" — made by the Church to the government during the Ancien Régime.

émigré
Those French people — notably the aristocracy and clergy — who left France during the Revolution. Many of them were counter-revolutionaries.

Enlightenment
The philosophical and intellectual movement of the 18th century that encouraged people to think for themselves on the basis of reason rather than through simple belief.

Estates General
The meeting of the three Estates called by the King and his government in May 1789 in an attempt to resolve France's problems. This event marked the beginning of the Revolution.

feudal system
The old social system that existed in France (and other countries) before the Revolution, in which the people had to fulfil many obligations to the nobility and the king.

Feuillant
A member of one of the more moderate Revolutionary groups. They wanted to form a constitutional monarchy where the king ruled with the agreement of the people.

Girondin	A member of a Revolutionary group that eventually argued for a Republic but was divided on whether the King should stand trial and be executed. A number of their leaders came from the department of the Gironde.
Hébertiste	A follower of the radical leader Jacques Hébert, the editor of the Père Duchesne, a newspaper popular among sans-culottes.
Indulgent	The name given to Danton and Desmoulins (and their followers), who towards the end of 1793 began to call for an end to "the Terror" and for mercy to be shown to prisoners of the Revolution.
Jacobin	A member of the Jacobin Club, originally a moderate organization but which became increasingly radical during the course of the Revolution. The Jacobins held their meetings in a former house of Dominican monks, who had been given the nickname of Jacobin friars from their first house on Rue Saint-Jacques.
maximum	Laws issued by the Revolutionary government in an attempt to fix prices (and later wages), in order to ensure economic stability and some degree of protection for the poorer people. The laws did not work well in practice, however, as prices continued to rise during the Revolution.
moderate	An individual or group wanting only a limited degree of change.
National Assembly	The first Revolutionary government, set up after the Tennis Court Oath in 1789 and lasting until the establishment of the Convention on 20 September 1792.
radical	A person or group believing in complete revolution, where the old organizations of the state, including the monarchy, were to be replaced.
Republic	A state or country governed by elected representatives of the people, and not by a king and his aristocratic followers.
sans-culottes	Workers, artisans and shopkeepers who were among the most radical supporters of the Revolution. Their name derived from the wearing of trousers and not the breeches (culottes) of the upper classes and nobility.
Socialism	A political theory and system in which all people have control and ownership of manufacture and trade. The French Revolution played an important role in the development of Socialism in the 19th century.
White Terror	A reaction to the excesses of "the Terror", when, following the fall of Robespierre, people attacked Jacobins and other radicals.

INDEX

PICTURE CREDITS

Jean-Loup Charmet/Bibliothèque Nationale
Paris/The Art Archive: 15
Jean-Loup Charmet/Musée Carnavalet
Paris/The Art Archive: 7, 21
Mary Evans Picture Library: 9, 16-17, 19,
27, 29
Dagli Orti/Musée Carnavalet Paris/The Art
Archive: 11